DREAM MUSEUM

VICTORIA, BRITISH COLUMBIA

DREAM MUSEUM

Liliane Welch

Copyright © 1995 by Liliane Welch

Canadian Cataloguing in Publication Data

Welch, Liliane, 1937-
   Dream museum

   Poems.
   ISBN 1-55039-056-2

   I. Title.
PS8595.E54D7 1995   C811'.54   C94-910972-X
PR9199.3.W44D7 1995

Publication financially assisted by the
Canada Council Block Grant Program

Published by
SONO NIS PRESS
1745 Blanshard Street
Victoria, British Columbia v8w 2j8

Designed, printed and bound by
MORRISS PRINTING COMPANY LTD.
Victoria, British Columbia, Canada

For Cyril

BOOKS BY LILIANE WELCH

POETRY

Winter Songs (1977) chapbook

Syntax of Ferment (1979)

Assailing Beats (1979)

October Winds (1980)

Brush and Trunks (1981)

From the Songs of the Artisans (1983)

Unrest Bound (1985) chapbook

Manstorna: Life on the Mountains (1985)

Word-House of a Grandchild (1987)

A Taste for Words (1988) chapbook

Fire to the Looms Below (1990)

Life in Another Language (1992)

Von Menschen und Orten (1992)

LITERARY CRITICISM

Emergence: Baudelaire, Mallarmé, Rimbaud (1973) with C. Welch

Address: Rimbaud, Mallarmé, Butor (1979) with C. Welch

PROSE

Seismographs: Selected Essays and Reviews (1988)

CONTENTS

I RENEGADE

Diptych 13

Winter Storm 14

November 16

Winter Morning 17

Pesto 18

Dolomite Splinters 19

Latin Truths 22

Moonlighting 23

Anticipations 24

Renegade 25

Our Names 26

Sentry 27

II VENETIAN LIGHT

Venetian Light 31

The Ginette Knaff Poems

Impressions of Venice 1990 35

Portal 36

"This is my language . . ." 37

Secret Wind 38

Times of Need 39

Seeing Canada through a Monotype-Collage 40

Painter's Youth   41

Toulouse Lautrec's Bed   44

Visiting Ben Heyart's Atelier   45

Underground North   46

The Miner   47

Summer Night   48

III   HUMAN DREAMS

Common Ground   51

For Kay Smith   53

E morta la scrittrice   54

Emily Dickinson and Walt Whitman   55

A Human Being?   56

The Classroom   57

The Bookstore   58

Rimbaud in Sackville   59

Rimbaud in Luxembourg   61

The West in 1992   62

Disneyland   63

Human Dreams   64

IV ACCOUNTS

Marriage Accounts   67
Ski Lift   68
Memories   70
Expedition Log   74
Deserted Gods   75
Last Train   77
Adieu   78
Dancer   79
Home   80
Life with Mother   82
Mama   83
Daughter and Father   84
Old Man   85
Dachau, Fifty Years Later   86

V JAZZ

Jazz   89
Luxembourgish Lesson   90
Afternoons at Namurs   91
Funeral in Meischdref   92
Laundry-Day at Mecher   93
River   94

On the Autobahn   95

Nuns in Clierf   96

Benedictine Prayer   97

Impressions of Vianden   98

Letter from Holland   100

Venerable Meals   101

VI   Twilight Toccatas   105
TWILIGHT
TOCCATAS

NOTES   113

ACKNOWLEDGEMENTS   115

CRITICS   117

I

RENEGADE

Diptych

Each August departure from Europe

Packing the suitcase, my feet remain
in Luxembourg's streets. It's busy, but the cafés
spill heady scents and light fires in restless heads,
summer spreading to a wide land of friendship.
Crowds herd the sidewalks all day. Bells,
palpable from the cathedral's roof, reclaim
what used to be real. Right here history flows,
a current carried by these blended silts,
blessed when cities cascade and families
go raspberry picking. At the Halifax airport
I shall forget this world like a dress
returned to its armoire. But its silks
will ravish me during January nights.
Canada's silence wrapped tight around me.

All winter in Canada

Surprises. Hallelujahs. Cups of wind.
Horizons to frighten us, or to beseech.
Days for islands, and for scrawled dreams.
Hours so weighted with golden coins
we walk knees bent, triumphant.
A cathedral navigating angels
and miracles home through the dark.
Dogs that take us to those woods, we might
never venture into. Open seas, the kind
that become souvenirs. Ice-motes in spring.
Worn out letters. Stories that travel alongside
a hidden river. Voices we pray to
but that remain in the trees. A people's magic and
necessary passwords, perhaps ours.

Winter Storm

On that January night
I waited in my study for a phone call,
Watching the blizzard close down our house
And thought about bashing the narcotic
Of conventional life—becoming a beggar,
A professional without special talents,
A conquistador discovering
A temple, gold fire in my mouth!—
Meanwhile on CBC
A Dr. Love cast melancholy over the room,
Reporting that despite mammographies
Breast cancer is epidemic
In the western world. Floodlights outside
Broke the snow
Into golden flecks that filled my eyes;
Alternately shaken by the snowplough's
Thud and the yellow lights refracting
The dark sky, my stare kept
The emptiness passable.

So I felt at home, with that winter storm,
Committing follies in the sanctuary of reason,
While steel prows swooshed
Big waves of whiteness over my mind.
Relaxed because I knew even the pheasants
Wouldn't work tomorrow in the woods,
All schools uninhabitable,
Three Maritime provinces on their duffs.
It made your joints dream
You were a bear wrapped in drowse,
Curled up to a partner
While your fur grew thicker
In the warm underground den.

That night, as the phone wouldn't ring,
During my search for heaven on earth,
Bridges between humans and beasts,
Changes of costumes and skin, I put on
My grandmother like a flying robe,
Trembled backward directly above the heart—
Her pewtery eyes called the roll of all dreams
Before holy images,
The wind, *enfant terrible*, grew fiercer . . .
I drifted through her low-lit rooms,
Cats asleep on cupboards, a warm wood stove,
Frugal meals, bells outdoors and inside
Voices spinning yarns about village
Scandals and intrigues. My fantasies
Circled her pastures, climbing into the sky,
The myths she lived, death at the window . . .

And as the phone call became
Entrapped in the voice of the storm,
My grandmother animated the house,
Like the windy cliffs of some peak's clouds,
Like the fever chart of endless tomorrows—
Like a surrender
To some other edge of risk.

November

Deep frosts bring out down shirts.
The last leaves straggle by and
a tricycle still lies on the lawn,
a coy Duchamp.

Tucked into sleep's thick fur,
the fetishes of summer recede.
A lone car creeps home
to quiet times
over ice-patched, empty roads.

You linger round the entrance
and push a cloth snake
against the door's draft.

November plots short steps
to the last suns
and turns, stares blankly,
as you vanish into subdued everyday.

Winter Morning

Coupled the crows sail
through dawn's immense cold—
Visitors requesting lodging
crowd the wild dark.
                      My heavy bones
measure the warm nest,
flannel sheets, a partner's leg.
Yet I rise:
the house still hums with nocturnal
"Who are we?", "Where are we?"
                            And the crows,
huge-beaked black comets,
track me to the kitchen
and pose as coffee
                before
they break free,
prophets and vagabonds.

Pesto

Today, epiphany or spring
so bright, I make a pesto sauce
and compose the lure of our Italian summers.
Snow, loss and age stay in Canada as
we plot escapes to the villa of Catallus, Garda Lake.

Here's a silence set on fire, ruins
of baths, wild flesh: massive. Offerings scattered
or received—rocks alive with lizards, Lesbia.
Stairways, desires between heart and sky.
Old stories and Sardo cheese, stables, pine nuts
sudden rain.

                      A friend pounds basil leaves
and serves us a pesto pungent and olive green.

Dozing

In the cities of Europe we are dozing beasts.
Clumsy bears, horses turning millstones.

Door

A huge blue door in the boil
of the cloudy sky. Dawn:
first light, the last milk
and quietude of night.

Buttress Veil

The Cima della Madonna clasps the Sass Maor
and their limestone heads
look at me
through the window. You are doing
stretch exercises. In my dreams
I climbed all night. Now
I pull on my boots. Sun,
icemelt, rocks crash
past the buttress veil.

Another Language

Dolomite alphabet,
another tongue:
our feet on the sky
study summits, in Italy
they start always with
C or S, Cima, Sasso.

Rainy Days

On the board game *Peak Experience*,
roombound, we live the Past Conditional,
what might have been, and icefalls
soar up like tall glass walls
in the old French railway stations
we ran through with heavy packs in the sixties.
The Alps beggared our hearts:
it was their grim epics
we had to face. I win,
reliving our last expedition
to Chamonix, how we left without climbing,
enraged. You want to read a book:
Calvino, his verbs quiet as doormice,
their tiptoe peeping from the page.

July 14

On the crest
of the Sasso d'Ortiga,
our jackets, gear.

Autumn frost.
I lead all the pitches up.
You lead all the rappels down.

Then

We feast at the Hotel Colfosco.
Peach brandy, it was a widespread day.

San Martino di Castrozza

Angelo and Egle count our ascents,
we spell them out. Peaks rise homeric
above San Martino, the mountain hamlet
living by sundials carved in stone.
Cimone Peak: an obelisk, a quartz lamp
dark red, and it calls us
by name, in the sentient fire
that becomes our North.

Latin Truths

In the Italy I harbour within
we're forever living summer afternoons,
descending a Jacob's ladder homeward,
the air ablaze with fatigue.
You are pensive, I am mute,
and above a sphinx broods.
Or maybe we're only a single pause between
surge and finale from a symphony.
We could abstain,
be flatlanders, like disk jockeys
hating silence, and then there would be only
the rapacious noise of a minor opera
over the void. But we favour Italy's
Latin truths, a vista where each summit knows
its name: the Cimone magnetizes infinity,
the Sass Maor solicits eternity.
How many life-times we spend there,
out of the world, invisible and free,
waiting for God's eye to glide over us.
Already the cooks in the valleys dream
steaming pasta, their amulet
against abandonment, while raconteurs
rise from love making and sleep.
But we want to be touched by rhythms
open and closed, the hands of the rocks
that sustained us all morning and
the trattoria where we eat each evening soup.

Moonlighting

When you flee to Italy
it improvises a classic
retreat with toasting friends
and a tang of privilege.
So the northern ethos gives over—
fortified faces to subversive wit,
potatoes and leeks to pasta and fruits,
misty forests to olive groves.
My Italy,
when it rises from the back stage of writing,
has only mountains, pilgrim poets,
our grandfather Rinaldo.
            It singles me out! *Simpleton*,
it calls, *stay away*.
The marketplace of nostalgia
holds few rewards.
Why moonlight with an Italy
if not to measure it against the true
home that governs us—our keepsake
we throw mindlessly from hand to hand,
its blessings dependable as clouds of rain.

Anticipations

How terrifying and concealed, what is coming.
This road vanishing
out of life, or the morning photo of Manstorna
on which the tiny cloud foretells
how a river of clouds mounts a parade,
how it will engulf us. You can envision
us on that peak: two tiny specks with packs
who thought ropes could tie the infinite.
We know now that only rappelling down void
into the unknown brings the magic
of salvation. That day
Sheila and Clarke were married
in Ontario, planting affection
onto each other's face. They only sensed
how silence must lean
over heaven. They planned
to boil luminous plum jam,
rake autumn leaves from their lawn.
They didn't hear the unspeakable, but skirting it,
were claimed briefly by the hand of tenderness.
They cruised only anticipations,
not the highway of fear
where Clarke was killed.
Alone in her garden today Sheila audits
the past: fifty tulips planted for
a husband lost. When she sees a vanishing road
it is distant and adrift, like Clarke.

Renegade

In the heart's summer
a long walk with God
up rock;

the mornings
turn wild,
the late twilights
stay underground.

Marmots harvest
alpine hay
for their winter dens.

Sentinels dream home
as eternal departure.

What will I become
or be?
Which solstice
breaking granite
to schist
will make me

the rebel angel
haloed by mica-flash?

Our Names

It's light, what we divine from our names
is light as snow-swirl and dandelion fuzz,
blossoms of the blank proscenium of God's eye.
Look closer, here grows the wild halo
of another life.

Sentry

Soon I shall migrate to the horizon—
disappear in the selves it must hide,
wander through an ancient light,
warm myself in its wildness.
I shall convene all my mountains:
those that brighten pages in books,
those whose rocks I ate, streams I drank,
those whose winds are still looking for me,
and the one I ascend now each day.
Its summit-wall rising
into the willingness for risk.
The climb outward
then inward opens a skylight to the ultimate
peak, known and unknown,
to a sentry approaching faster,
bolder, than I can sing.

II
VENETIAN LIGHT

Venetian Light

A friend wrote recently, "For all artists
Born up north, Venice will always be
    A powerful tonic—Only there can they
Feast on the choreography of light . . ."
    The letter mapped my own desires
        Not only because I seek
The Italian spell during winter captivity
    As aurora borealis lifts Canadian nights.
And not because the Adriatic breezes
    Waft the pungent fantasies of
        Olive oil, pastas, bread.
Nor just that in Venice sins settle gently
    On the canals like a flock of white geese . . .
No, it's that I wake summer mornings and see
    On the wall opposite my Luxembourg bed
Dawn brush the dimness from
    Knaff's aquarelle *Impressions of Venice*,
The thick-chested, square-jawed,
    Sexual-faced palazzi
Billowing up their black lacy scarves,
    The fluid sweep of greys
        Nudging that lone ochre flare
Into conspiratorial waters.

      Last Christmas I read the German
Version of Brodsky's *Watermark*. Islanded with
  That bearish Russian sniffing clever Italians,
The hunter's archaic intimacy with prey . . . And
    The German captured me, its atavistic sounds
      Plumbing my ears, all else periphery,
And deep within the grip of its beats,
    Almost like the turbulence of a bazaar's human
      River revealing stillness,
I could smell, in the shoals of the hazy
    Laguna of silence, in its passageway,
      Frozen seaweed—
This October, when I read in English Brodsky's
  Annual Christmas romance with Venice—
Flights of an exile's paradise on the page—
     I savoured fully the mediated city of the sea,
Its name laced with Knaff's colours and lines,
    Its waters vibrant with German words
      And English images.
Then its skies shaped by twilight winds
    Pushed a rush . . .
       Of adrenalin into my Venetian dream.

The Ginette Knaff Poems

AFTER HER AQUARELLE AND FIVE MONOTYPES

Impressions of Venice 1990

The way a fervent medieval scribe
Loving light torches the virgin page,
Blues, gold and reds
That he explodes into a ball of fire,
Bright flesh he fingers and venerates
In Norwegian silence,
Until he has brought heaven to earth,
Illumined God's eye with his splendour;
So her blacks, greys and whites
Stand on the Lido with an ochre wind
In their hair, and swirl Venetian
Shapes, lines, a palette of echoes
To swim past our eyes—the way
A fleet of gondolas glides through fog.
As the dark palazzi track mythic treasures
Across sands, the Adria beats in us.
Chiaroscuro jubilates. Aschenbach's death,
Pound's vibrato. Fathoms beckon.
Vivaldi conjures spring and fall
With the silk hangings of time. Her aquarelle
Restores eternity, as ancient murals reclaim
A wilderness dazzled
And tamed. The hush of permanence, a caress.

Portal

It could be the door in a narrow Venetian street,
its wood suspicious from old assaults, and nobody home—

no geography alive behind the black panels,
the ancient stories
silent on their murals;

and yet sometimes (the doorjamb's ochre
permanence, the wall's warm greys shiver)
a shy sentry joins
expectations, from beyond this barrier,

from the hallway's maze
behind the entrance, through
further rooms and lives:

a forgotten welcome from melodies,
as if a saxophone or an unseen saint
issued a timeless morse.

Inscribed on this portal, a bonfire
that shifts its dark wing. Why wait
before a painting? Is it a gate
for a tentative visit home?

"This is my language . . ."

A painting like a boxcar
Stacked with summer days. The painter lingering
Near the door sees the world spread before her,
An exigent beauty. Or the old prince invoking memories.
The racy Italian underwear that his lover
Conceals under
Her austere words, the erotic gestures when
She washes crystal Venetian goblets.
What a subtle, romantic homage, and
That young woman restoring with perfect repose
A Caravaggio in an island house near Sirmione,
Time suspended, Catallus asleep. Now the old nobleman
Recounts his anecdotes: Safaris perhaps,
But certainly he recalls the triumphs of some war,
Or a few peaks conquered, and the past shudders
Through him as pleasure. As a boxcar opened on the plains.
The world! Those rapacious reds,
Those yellows like golden legs flashing
Under white dressing gowns.
The blues miss desire's lighthearted anarchy.
Or the greys vibrant with ceremonial discretion.
Close the boxcar. Hang the painting on your wall.

Secret Wind

Through the skylight (a latticed pulse) the spring wind
impatiently—not because wonder and grace
        sleep, but because dreams, now,
        swollen from such long nights
        of bondship,
        besot us indolently—
enters to circle the greys of sullenness, each tunnel
of that stuffy lair, the heart's
black troughs, upright bars.

It hangs a museum in the sky, changes
hollow places—a ruby eye to translate
desire, silks to blindfold despair;
but tunes already the lips of storms
in a velvet dark we yearn for and recall.

Times of Need

As if we were waiting—lost children
of a mute age, of a dark forest,
our heads speckled discs flown deeply into loss,
the altar before us drawing all eyes, its flares
feathery orange as it strives upward,
tremulous, in amazement, from the restless hopes
steadily gathering and retreating.
                        Then we perceive
a hint of the light massed far away,
a light both holy and cold. We can endure its iron winter,
we're fire lovers. And we do. We'll burst
into praise, having stalked the divine so long.
Light the compass
for trekking through times of need, for expecting
an altar's concealed God, present or fled.

Seeing Canada through a Monotype-Collage

It burns me, the lava
of a sun escaping a dark bed
rising from mud, a bold laughter
as when a knife peels
our hands and our words
search the heart, where it seems
distant icons breathe and so awaken
new starts. Your work
lifts the dresses of silence
between us, and I wonder
if images are the windy fields
which hold our lives together,
our old and new worlds.
Snatching the eye, a postage stamp
taken from one of my letters, missives
that walk off those harsh winters,
visions I share often
with you. Lustred by frost
an arrow feathers the unknown,
the window of a joy endless,
the one you kindle from
the northern land I love.

Painter's Youth

On the chessboard
near the town library
we talked about our teachers
who devoured books, concerts,
paintings for their memoirs,
our parents who furnished
their modest, grey days with
earthly things, make-believe still lifes.
Often we wandered
through petty events, past
slate-covered roofs and sculptures
of gossip, the minutia
primordial in a small
mining town, radiators
and guardians of morality
rattling behind brick façades.
You hated the insignia
of affluence and dreamed about Paris
where painters worked in garrets
and women didn't wear
girdles or grim faces
but fireworks of perfume.
Painting was omnipresent
for you even then.

You wanted to preserve the sun's lava,
not the heavy blow of God's hand;
a crumb of goodness,
not the zeal of priests
who seasoned spring with bile;
unbridled fantasm in ultramarine,
luminous red, bursting yellow,
not the posed monodrama of despair.

You were unfaithful to our homeland,
its trees, mines, clouds,
called it a middle class
brothel with bigoted procuresses,
meaty libertines, muzzled lust.
The Provence spoke to you better,
calls of encores from artists,
philistines wintering in limbo
and a demimonde receptive
as hell, an oasis emitting
lavender, sage and saffron smells.

There you were going to make it.
Break the code of colours,
paint an earth intensified and
swollen, a precipice of alchemy,
unimaginable lights.
So strolling amidst the pink cheeked,
stout legged northern women
you had left already for the south.

Fragments of Grimm, psalms of learning
were still then in my ears,
and when one afternoon I saw
your hand stroking a woman's thigh,
the visible world was not multiplied,
I thought of copulating dogs.

Last time when I returned home
they told me you were dead.
The shouts of your last tableaux,
deadly reds and rending blues,
were the predators chasing you
to a darkness where the whiplash
of abandonment fell onto your bare skin.

I have often been to your France.
Talked with your first woman at Les Baux.

Toulouse-Lautrec's "Bed"

I often wonder
about love and the Lord
who invades my sleep to save
and devastate it. I could
ban him to the cellar,
but am tempted
by closed eyes, fingers restless
as midnight's longing for
the first sun.—How strange
to drive strength into a lack,
but winter mornings the pillows
exhale forgotten visions,
voices, promises,
the pink tongues of stillness.
Perfumes of obscure apparitions
arrive and the intense reds
in Lautrec's painting incite me
to fathom moments of touch
that are spiral staircases into heaven
and show God's face beyond
its distant moats.
Camping thus outside desire
I enter eternity. I am
one of the heads under the quilt.
Within the serene warmth
of worn affection, I recompose
the riddle of love in servility's bed.

Visiting Ben Heyart's Atelier

His paradise:
    forest floors wide open.
The paints—a symphony's
    major key—tend
trees, invisible beasts that
    crouch in the brush,
deep odours that
    pulse from the ground.
Inspecting his atelier
    scours dailiness,
presages incantations,
    snow lighting up
the winter nights.

Here we rapture
    in colours wide-eyed,
yearn for rocks,
    praise the earth's signature
strung as massive beads
    over the walls,
hunger for blessedness,
    splinters of sky.

Underground North

BEN HEYART'S WOODCUT *FEMME FAILLE*

Woman, enshrined in a trunk: silhouette
thirsting for hot light,
bedded omega,
earth witch
retrieved by probing hands—

as if caresses could release
your sinews, sanctify
your bark house!

        Wood,
(vessel, hieroglyph, crack)
dizzy stir of Merlin's sleep, pivot
your grain like a cauldron
and aim us toward a door—
love—

    you will hold us in your alcove,
innocent and asking if idols
can mate with stones and gods,
wood-muse, underground north
toward which our eyes sail.

The Miner

EMILE HULTEN'S SCULPTURE IN ESCH

Solemn and sovereign, all year round, where
a black river of cars whirls between
dusty façades with shutters rusted open,
he stands in his heavy boots watching.
He has plodded out of the mines
still hoarding ore from long ago.
His hands carve the hills of this city's story,
red underground sanctum closed now.
Luxembourg steers toward
the bankers' moneyed night as he inspects
his stone one. Is he forgotten, with his lamp?
On this spring day, he sees himself
embrace the earth's cool womb—daily journeys
into darkness to open the sky for an entire land.
And is rewarded:
young sightseers, invisible all winter,
surround his pedestal, breathe in
astounded his stillness,
are sustained by a life of toil.

Summer Night

Between sky and mesa, Georgia O'Keeffe,
austere, remote, free, priestess of colours,
danced with the wind. Her long black dress
loosely billowing concealed
a mysterious summer night.
She needed only desert gifts. A white touch
near the nape sent messages
clear as March frosts; the gaze
was crazed with stillness. Trophy
of America's great art days,
at ninety she still played
the young girl from Little Rock.

She was the black door.
Constant in *The Patio*
looking forever toward that perfect
blue against which our erotics
will be a mere chalky pelvis
amidst wild sage.

III
HUMAN DREAMS

Common Ground

In San Martino, the doors of the peak
walls unlock veering wind blasts,
clouds sweeping anguish and fears,
our intimacy with the rocks like keys
jangled by silence. The sacred is still alive.
We climb impatient, play Titans,
without hedge taste the shiver
of dawn and risk, then I remember
your letters, magnetized by
expeditions through Fredericton bookstores,
leaping crevasses of ephemera,
craving the overhangs of poetic screes.
You have fjords, jungles, chasms,
glaciers in the bones, working your garden,
that Eden thick, inedible, bright.
A pleasant enough existence when one isn't
contemplating the intemperate heart and
empty head of humanity, you say.
Each letter a tall glass of soda
fizzing with New Brunswick miniatures.
In the Dolomites I perform devotions
to stone gods, bewitched by their secret
syncopes and take steps
forbidden to valley feet.

From each peak bursts your
1990 Christmas greeting: *Peace
on earth—if not to the animals,
nor to us, to beauty, which abides all things!
Though we attack and destroy it repeatedly.*
I leave the mountains for the eastern province,
where other vertical barriers wait
and the soul, acrobat over void,
misses sometimes a partner's grasp,
summer ascents only memory now.
San Martino, Sackville, New Brunswick—
our common ground where
the sky is empty of rock magic
and melancholy knocks at the gate
winter nights, questioning like
a psalmist who has forgotten his song.
*Some days I'm just glad for the wind,
continue to be wild.*

For Kay Smith

Lucent wings pinned tight
to their backs, the gold haloes scattered

on the writing desk. Your words have flown out,
and eloped with the old sea lions

beyond Fundy Bay. In their hands silver
flutes and drums. A nun leaves her life.

Morning, the gulls. The kingfisher
dropping for prey. Lips

on the waves, the prayers of summer rain.
A prophet waking to the wine in the song

he hums. Dear Kay, with the loneliness
of winter, and the new affections learned

in Homer; with a loon's heady laughter,
and the desire of a seal; the accordion of shale,

its puckered silence; with the lift of snow geese,
and the beds of wetlands—with these,

you'll draw new coasts,
the sea changes, rock shifts,

as the tides boil our lives. The sonnets
and troubadours, Kay; the lovely world.

"E morta la scrittrice, aveva 75 anni"

"THE WRITER IS DEAD, SHE WAS 75"

On the photo Natalia Ginzburg
fixes a clear eye onto the world.
Her mouth, smileless, fled
the satisfied table of family life
to live on coffee and eggs,
unable to drink florid words.
No typewriter cluttered her table,
her pen alone battled against small talk.
Her travellers, bridge players, movie goers
bury their thoughts in chatter,
kill silence on each page.
She accepted winter and exile.
Betrayed by her body,
she speaks now the language of stillness,
while we search for a pass-key
to escape houses filled with unnamed pain.
How her sober voice still resounds,
without pathos, without lies.

Emily Dickinson and Walt Whitman

Behind her sealed wall
in Amherst Emily writes:
How public—like a frog—
To tell one's name—the livelong June—
To an admiring bog,
while Walt *never made*
to live inside a fence
celebrates himself as *Kosmos,*
turbulent, fleshy, sensual.
Even from his massive tomb in Camden
he takes possession of the world,
sings: *I give myself,*
grows body-leaves.
Emily trembles and thinks:
how dreary to be Somebody.

A Human Being?

Driving into the interior
of an Elizabeth Bishop poem
you become *the worst gardener since Cain*
while the rocks break with light, you ask,
Why am I a human being?
and hear Debussy faintly play.

The Classroom

He thought he liked the outdoors—
and became a teacher.

Penetrated the wood's source.
The wild he lived in first with Hopkins
then Thoreau: canoetrips past slimed cliffs;

staring at his class—rigid, dutybound,
      the room—roadless as a mudhole,
      the pupils—mindless in their deadness,
         not even rutting;

still
he prowls briefly
through texts: thickets
streaming towards light.

In a dark suit
he waits to pull on
his mask.

The Bookstore

Assembled by winters, decades, pioneers,
a world still safe. Houses wedged into hills
to meet the Fundy gales. Marshes wistfully dyked,
churches quaint and snug, circling heavenward.
Chocolate of tidal bore, slate-grey of sky.
A postcard pastoral. Uphigh a college
scatters to the townlette its seeds of culture.
The proud flèche of its chapel,
scoffed at or revered, christens strollers
with nostalgic imperatives; the massive façades,
sandstone red, of the library more urgent
today than when books reigned. And all erected
not upon scholars alone but through the work
of others' faith—preachers, rich patrons.
The art gallery, above all,
refurbished, underlines an emptiness—
or its icons do, a lack slowly forgotten.
But perhaps not. In a brown shed, almost hidden,
the textbook depot. Deemed:
"A warehousing concept that works well"
by accountants. We can neglect
straying over there. No bookstore
on this campus, a town orphaned.

Rimbaud in Sackville

Last March, with Rimbaud,
The student walked over the dykes
Hearing the icefloes break
On the murky Atlantic waters
And toyed with slipping away,
Unmooring his life—becoming
A jazz musician or a legionnaire,
Travelling to St. Petersburg or Siberia
Into the Russian mind.—
And "The Drunken Boat"
In his pocket opened as flyway
Before a bird's skyward sweep.
Just then scholars all over the world
Were celebrating the hundredth anniversary
Of the great writer's death.

So the student clasped his breviary,
Rimbaud's slim *Oeuvre*,
Sharing his sailings
To the unknown.
Because the French poet was a free,
Absolved spirit, buffeted by
Drifts and storms. An accomplice
Whose compass pointed so intensely
Elsewhere you wanted to be with him
Mad for the sea washing you of all stain,
Knowing the oceans by heart.
And why not give yourself to a poet,
Who indicted the impure fathers
and mothers of poetry?

Last March, as the student wrote at his desk,
Turned to the last blizzard,
To the pale squalls, to three crows perched
On the belfry across his yard,
He wanted to eat the stones of that church
And the entire campus—
It was Satan snoring under cover of
Eloquence, knowledge encased in
Empty cradles, obscene hearses.
He opened *A Season in Hell*,
When shall we go beyond the mountains
And shores to greet the birth
Of new labours, new wisdom, the flight
Of tyrants, demons, the end of superstition
To adore Christmas on earth?

He pondered this,
And the spruces whipping
The last erotic edge, the rush of winter.
Rimbaud's *Illuminations*, in his head,
Silent and transparent
Like the white June nights up north.
You could walk without shadow
Over their roads, hear only
Your boots pounding the ground.
And slowly, as the winds
Searched the emptiness outside,
The student's thoughts threw off their shawls
And fur coats, they danced
Like the bright air of vine and lemon blooms.

Rimbaud in Luxembourg

> *Et war esou em d'Paischten*
> *'t stung alles an der Bléi*

Pentecost morning, promised tongues flare.
The fetishes of work fade.
Young Gérard wants to be Rimbaud.
Rapt he worships a stanza,
doesn't hear the churchbells,
sounds he otherwise profanes.
Celestial calls blight *"j'irai loin,*
bien loin, comme un bohémien."
Down below his father waters
the garden: deep green potatoes
framed by blooming flowers.
Bored with well-ordered life, Gérard
plucks the digitalis from Rimbaud's *"Fleurs."*
A band, somewhere up the street,
is playing the Hammelsmarsch, nostalgia
for farmers in blue smocks amidst sheep.
Drums throb and throb.

The West in 1992

As if Mark were a hermit
forever in his cell, sleeping with
saints from prayers barely heard,
angels from poems hardly read,
his hands like wind chimes
raised in the sea breeze . . .

No, Mark's in Los Angeles
—that last purgatory, folly of malls and cars—
busy in smog. With his house-mate,
the ageing biker, Mark thirsts
for tenderness, not sins
at a stripper's house, relearns guitar,
and edits the memoirs
of a former Balkan queen.
His eyes full of summer aureoles:
Jasper, where he feels most alive,
peaks winter white, valleys autumn bronze,
grizzlies besotted by berry covered slopes.
Dreams of November: Baja rituals,
whales mating in cold Pacific salts—
Or Mark conjures redemption, at last,
camped on a thin dolomite strip
in the bristlecone pine reserve
amidst nine thousand year old trees.

Disneyland

Disneyland throbbing outside dreamless L.A.—
who is more alone
             than the white man
saying, "Honey, this is great!"
        to a tanned wife?
convinced, since his kid is happy,
the crowd in transports of frolics,
and restaurants bursting with mouths,
      that even the Indians
should leave their reservations
             to help out Mickey Mouse.

"You ask me to work the soil.
   I would have to
   cut off my mother's
breast. When I die
she will no longer take me in . . . To cut
   the grass, to make hay.
      How would I dare cut my mother's hair?"
a Cherokee answered Jefferson long ago.

Human Dreams

It was like a park full of skaters, yes . . .
Like that pond of Breughel, spinning peasants
    I saw one day in a Dutch museum,
Ice of the first cold nights suddenly on the tongue.
    I felt the stillness of winter play, far from
        Foggy lecture halls, cloudy churches.
A heaven with angels gambling away haloes,
    Saints tearing the incense from their face.
God's bed was empty, his eternal monogamy with
    Virtue broken; vows of constancy gone;
No more restrained strolls through paradise.
    A daemonic lust had roused him, to dance
between the swords of erotics, swallow an arsenal
    Of poisons. On his throne, granite tablets
    Like a huge illumined tome
Proclaimed new laws, his needs
    So wild they seemed a fiery core,
Their nomadic letters streaked across the page
    In a measureless orgy. At his kingdom's gate,
    A pirate flag, hoisted, unfolding
Immoralist exploits, sacked altars,
    Desacralized shrines—the detonations of
His power sinking the mast of all norms;
    In the constellations, the heathen
Freedom one sees in southern men, devoid of
    Winter fears. All human dreams
    Forever on the road to Damascus
Roiled up by art . . . his wind, its music,
    Its eruptions whipping our boats,
        Our safely coiled ropes,
Onto dangerous journeys, the last ocean of play.

IV
ACCOUNTS

Marriage Accounts

He will remember the entire desert's eye
loving with fury two oasis dwellers;

but she will speak of ancient times, Herodotus,
the zone between legend and land,

vast, silent pocket of history bearing
fables, mirages and caravans—

a marriage of disappeared, reappeared
courtship sailed into by two nomads,

an eclipse where
books became her door

into a kingdom with sky.
And she will remember

how she could have led him through
sandstorms five thousand years ago,

slipped down centuries
to charts with secret wells,

but how he desired only fire and sand,
his face hooded against her invented world.

Ski Lift

Although the professor mutters *escape*,
swallowing it slowly like an espresso,
and his wife decides, *happiness perhaps*,
both wonder. They are on a ski lift
swooping through forest lanes,
mist stretching up
to the sky's grey seam.
Their down mittens clasp the tow bar.
He is lost in the poem "Movement"
and tells her Rimbaud walked over
these Alps on his way south.
Steel masts punctuate the exposed slopes,
the snap of the wheels above.
They watch young people,
brightly clad angels, mark
the distances of some white tapestry—
plunge to another depth.

He connects again with Rimbaud's
visions: fantastic processions
foreshortened like a page torn.
The broken script crowded
by learned sounds.
On both sides of the lift skiers
race lines, clues
down the icy expanse.
His wife next to him nudging
him from his cerebrations.
That afternoon, he finds her buried
in drifts, two hands flailing
from a coffin of snow.

With snow flurries, the phrase
*inventions of the unknown demand
new forms*, dogging him.
Entwined in the notations
left on his desk, for hours he rides up
and down, waiting for the sun to burn
through and compensate for the sadness
of being a scholar.

Memories

Three decades later and as the olive
air and ripe tomatoes swell
in the summer night, he remembers Megan
here, in the animated streets
of Perugia, echoes of voices
among the Corso's houses, thick espresso smell,
sun-slabs straight down, his words
planting lust into the light
as he heard her mating the sounds
of Italian with Anglo-Saxon reverence,
the passion in her eyes like a gold
stone, those months of her studies
at the institute for foreigners. She fled
into his sun-trapped culture, the shudder of centuries,
urged on by the barrens of her homeland.
He was longing too then, as her eyes roved
over the darkness of Etruscan graves
that stored moonlight for her. In the ecstasy
of immersion, she began to smoke
and to eat with him each noon
in a town of palazzi and marble gleam.
Retrace a foreign culture
and all antecedents
will track you everywhere:
you'll be the root in a dry August
reaching for receding waters,
the shriek of a cicada over parched land,
stalking a procession long faded.
She spoke often of Virgil,
with whom he had to take
many forced walks as an adolescent,

the tradition in that conqueror's name,
the untiring desire to maintain a heritage.
In Paris, his wife said, there were cafés,
winter days, movies and French men with
foreign female students who lived together.
In Padua she told him there was only the longing.
Women students from good Italian
families remained virgins.
Italian cities, dreams cast in stone
jailing their dwellers, the melancholia
of men attached to their mothers' skirts.
Then, his heroes were Hemingway, vital
vagabonds, not exorcized
by introspection, athletes of action
who sought out, enjoyed simple things;
like Mark Twain he didn't want
Michel Angelo for breakfast, lunch,
dinner, tea, supper and for between meals.
He had not yet met Megan, the flax-haired girl
from America, not yet dreamed
departure through her.
But she left, he stayed behind, later
married an Italian wife. The literature
of America with its prism of a new man
no longer rainbowed his days.
Now as he walks with the other men,
back and forth in the streets each night,

he helps them build a word-house
for two lodgers, Casanova
downstairs and Tristan upstairs
and only wants the misty blue of Megan's eyes.
He discards the Mediterranean
role as paterfamilias where he respects
his wife, is loyal to house, home
and caring for his two sons.
Once he stole a handkerchief
from Megan's purse, to keep
her smell near his face at dawn
when the owls' calls pierced the sky.
Always when he met her she was elsewhere
in Rome's catacombs pouring over diaries
of bones, in a Pinacoteca loving
Renaissance paintings, in her journal
where vacancies of the heart
resonated through urns and she wrote:
I want to change
my life, discover something
important about our past.
He recalls his honeymoon near Garda Lake
when the dark, fashionable woman,
his wife, created the first strategies
to accept a husband's infidelities.
Later as they visited Catullus' villa
she invented her talent for motherhood
and began her devotion to him: nods,
smiles, agreement, ways to keep him near;
with the air of a Contessa she would never
shun him for failing her.

He recalls the stars falling
through those deceptions and the bells of several
churches rang the quarter hours. Right then
tenderness became a fall into subterfuge,
marriage a long sleepless night.
He teaches now at the institute for foreigners
where he once risked everything and Megan said:
true love resides in the house of memory,
memory to light up passion's code,
memory to link present and past,
memory to dilate desire,
to recover the wild.
On the ship over Garda Lake, water
shattering in green spray on the hull,
he avoided hearing the swell
of the secret undersong.
In a New England library's
books about Pompeii,
in the heaviness of old truths,
in the lowlands of learned journals,
in a house where perhaps
a husband waits, on travels
through Europe where she shields
her eyes from Perugia,
he refigures Megan's present life.
There is a river of promises between
him and that world, and this side,
idolater he waits, shovels
his memory open to overtake
the morning of sadness
with a silence older than bliss.

Expedition Log

It is late Fall on Broad Peak
and Edo is huddling in a storm-bound tent

writing his expedition log.
The avalanches have not yet swept the giant's head.

Dear friend, one page says,
where the North Face soars into dream

ice-fluted buttresses are my home.
I eat the wind's creations

when I sleep. How long since I looked
at store windows along city streets.

Returned home
I might forsake my wife and child,

we don't imagine the same skies.
My friend, can mountain men love other humans?

Between peaks and women,
they'll always take the peaks.

We yearn to be clouds hugging the gods.
I talk with every sunbeam and gale.

The mountain's slopes are crystal
honeycombs, its breath a terrifying call.

Deserted Gods

A woman in a kitchen, ears aroused,
responsive to voices, hands pounding dough,
face flared with untold choreographies.
Those wide eyes
spiralling with larks some days,
swarming with stars at night,
are love's fossils, stern and visionary.
The woman has slipped into motherhood—
tempted sometimes not to leave its contentment;
that safe plodding through valleys
far from windy crests.
Owned by a man, their sons.
Owned by a name, a metaphor
for partnership, and the shadow of words folded
into a closet. But in that straw basket
she lives like a bird,
sunless and godless days,
rainbowed only by "when the kids
are gone I'll get back to writing again";
or remembering
from a radio song the intimacy
she had as a girl with words.
She meets this old self now
on occasionally sacred bridges.
This woman perhaps,

at thirteen, slaying the Hydra of babble
in her parents' home, and even more
at school with nuns; a girl always
putting her cheek against the sound of poems.
She stripped them bare, felt their skin.
Her life continues now
the man depending on her
with a daily domain and the other
self, wearing sackcloth and ashes—
and also her oldest boy, hung out on
the limb of youth as over a whirlpool
with the faces of her deserted gods.

Last Train

She felt a shudder
under her feet
when, at sunrise, the train came for her
at seventy five—

As a girl, at funerals, she held on to her hat,
supplicant to the wind which swallowed
the priest's words; and the tombstones rose elliptic,
transitory grails, she saw
swarming out of the ground, and
wouldn't understand.

Before her own last voyage, she again
paced the glowing vineyards of youth.

Old offender! Had she not acknowledged
           volatility from champagne?
           Learned goodbyes?
           Releasement?
She's foolish forever!
And consumed by fires still
like a stubborn star drinking darkness.
She tries to forget. Her eyes glittering
from an ancient faith, a fugitive horizon
that toasts the present, receding in disbelief,
as the last train tunnels near.

Adieu

Mornings in an empty house, her name now
Echoing elsewhere,
                      in some stone cellar.
Subdued, October's muted suns
Placing memories on long shadows.

What do we burrow through?
                                  Her dominion of welcomes—
Eighty-five years bevelled by work,
An armoire full of linen nightshirts, tablecloths
Amidst lavender sachets.

We remove a key from its hook behind the door,
Repossess ancient books.
                        On a photograph
We reach for her lips.

Dancer

As she reaches for an arabesque
In flight, her feet seize nothing
But the spell of boards shining and spinning.

And then her mother's fixed eyes uttering,
"L'Etoile!—Degas would paint your flutter,
Gathered, perfected, a comet's tail."

And she herself, like a dandelion, wants
To stand submerged in a field, her up-turned
Face above roots held firm.

Home

Victoria flees each summer to the city
to Toronto, and then rents
fiercely a room as though
she were a paladin somewhere
in that legendary battle called
"Escape from home," where
the tribal structure is
feudal, and her father
hastening through the house generates
awesome obedience from everyone.
Breathless she watches his dominion
and impact on her now silent mother.
"I never understood it," her grandmother says,
"your mother wears patience."
No, Victoria can't believe it, histrionic
triumph over a woman once
the Joan of Arc amidst peers,
her fervid worship of that condottiere.
She has grappled with distaste
but she returns each fall.
His tactical genius culminates in
victims succumbing to an eloquent
veneer, and she feels enfeebled
like a phantasm in winter
left to merge with the bloodstained mist.
She defects to nightlife all summer,

becomes a stray cat
stalking the drone of bars,
claustrophobic behind a face
carefully made up, always travelling
with backward looks.
How to return, home, drugged,
thinking that you belong there,
peering through blood ties, a curtain
stiff as frozen sheets,
the grandfather clock ticking,
cinnamon scent in each room?
Should she or not? She's
searching, intent upon finding
the fleeting happiness of life. Forgotten
the narrows of liberation,
the lovers in her summer diet,
crossing herself with survival
and fantasies hung in the sky.
Do mountains want to be moved?
She sees the nightly wilderness
linking another handcuff to the wrist,
she feels her unleavened rebellion
reach a heaven blank or
a masquerade of veterans adrift.
At dawn she can absolve the patriarch.

Life with Mother

She shared her life with him on secret rendez-vous
told him about piano playing, sewing
a dog who patrolled loneliness.
Days might pass without violent weather
arctic light straining at her serenity
and then a hurt from long ago
would find now some home in her middle years.
She promised to move in with him.
She lived with her mother behind
soft window lights, spotless
mirrors and floors, varnished woodwork
and a secluded garden geometrically shaped—
male gods banned from the kingdom
of clipped hedges, the maternal eye protecting
a windless refuge dwindled to missed connections.
She told him later in a country café
Sunday crowds, picnickers on the river banks
that her desires were suspended
beneath that Roman-nosed mother.
My childhood was unspent, she said.
One August evening she rang his doorbell
holding a large envelope frayed on top.
The hurt she murmured, but remained outside.
On the threshold they looked at a glossy photo.
See how she triumphs insouciant.
A woman in black
tearing down a kite, with the tutored
hand of a bear.

Mama

For years aching that the son
she loved so much (and could not release
to any other woman)
would leave:
              her life-giving child
eating pasta slowly evenings at the table
in her small, spicy kitchen,
satisfied, comfortable—
then suddenly overnight,
the change to a married man
in bed with a wife, naked as when
his young body would step into the bath
to be scrubbed and dried before he stretched
for the maternal arms, would now kiss
the nipples of that woman, fascinated,
anointed by the oils of her eyes.
For years aching; having to ache
because he no longer held her hand.

Daughter and Father

Enduring day, awaiting night
her father
at eighty-nine

always composed now,
smiles to talk hoarsely,
drag his feet
and plunge into the past,
that deep well of war between them,
his bony, curved back a falcon's
without the blazing wrath.
Copper-tinted hands bridge
the sadness of time.
                        Patience,
peace, penitence
are caravans sent him by twilight;
the silent dunes engulf him;
and the oasis where he will be
bedouin and king, she defusing
old minefields
strewn in the sand
when he is gone.

Old Man

My daughter recalls me
as the sinister lord
from her youth.
I conjure my daughter
as a sentinel
of tolerance, devotion,
when I can't or won't rise
from bed or refuse to talk,
on dark days,
envying her
youth, the years she has
left to redeem me.

Dachau, Fifty Years Later

"Lord, release him!"
                          The daughter's lips
waken to despair, the flames
that are her father's presence,
his life sentenced to a desert's face,
rocks ridged by night, his absence.

Darkness, his vanishing;
                          the daughter's lips
stoking through soot. Like a log
in a ceramic stove—
blaze, silence, blackened
bones. Ashes!

A father tortured in this camp.
                          The daughter's lips
scorched, terror still ebbs and flows,
silence shrouds him. Suffering
revives him. The daughter
grasping the flames.

V
JAZZ

Jazz

Winter nights, cosy
kitchen, shutters closed, unknown worlds
inside the radio box. Jazz recasting
the room, heady clarinets on
clear waters of joy.
A teenager impassioned by that force.
And cracks of the trumpets blasting
sweet enough to flee.
Beyond the Atlantic
America showered sounds
on the mining town, a quicksilver rain,
dionysian. Jazz,
its outbursts went right
to your bones, pulsed mellow
dances through your head,
with fluid saxophones that made
you fly, trombones
flinty like granite peaks,
and the drums whorled
me away from days of unused love.
Firing me beyond control, jazz
uncaged great animals,
waterfalls on winter evenings
in Luxembourg, in my parents' house,
jubilant through my girlhood,
kept the beat alive.

Luxembourgish Lesson

They meet on a winter night.
The teacher is sibyl
in an ocean of windswept words.
And the students—slowly tranced
by a river of unknown sounds,
ford pools, ponds, floods.
This schoolroom is timed to dreams.
The students' lips join with her mouth
as sailors, but already,
swept into a torrent of delight,
she steers toward deeper waters.
Their grown-up voices unroll
the verbs of her mother tongue
as it breaks in spume.
She has urged many migrants seaward;
this spring she will fly to the Bahamas,
ride higher surfs.
They too yearn for blessings, their eyes,
stained with long workdays,
sight misty islands, cottages
on the Moselle's vine-covered banks.

Afternoons at Namurs

She was still young,
in her late twenties,
when she put on weight.
Did she simply open
the doors of her mind
to the melodies of cakes? And
did she look forward
mornings while cooking
to Namurs where the cream puffs
waited to travel through her body
like the shooting stars she had
expected at night,
at whose tables
her girl friends waited,
coaxing each other to eat
more tarts as the afternoons twirled
slowly in the streets
outside the gourmet palace
and the inside buzzed festive
with the shrieks of women
fat enough to perform as circus freaks?
What self streamed through her
at those crossroads? And when
she returned home to eat
supper with her husband
who had stayed lean,
went jogging twice a week,
did she navigate
her torso with guilt,
her huge fingers
aching for the Belgian chocolates
performing ballets in the pastry shop
where the women were wed to words and sweets?

Funeral in Meischdref

All birds shut down
Onto the coffin poured a steady rain
The priest wrapped
With incense consoled the family
Blessed Jemp's remains.
His agony ghosted on the cemetery walls.

How past the Nazi slaughter house
Through Tambow's endless muds
Some thousand young Luxembourgers hibernated
With fear, starved underground
Dim abandoned shapes
Remembered another world
Stared homeless into Russia's eyes:
Unfathomable woods, snow deserts, madness, and
Nights Jemp leading their prayers
"Virgin Mary guide us home"
And during two years many survived.

While the requiem draped praise across death
We recalled a good man
Wept a lost saint
His silence sang in mournful hymns
The bells now wordless
As his Tambow comrades gave a last salute.

Then at the burial feast, grief
And joy tangled brightly as flowers.
A whole village, honed to Jemp's absence,
Begot laughter from loss
With ham and pinot gris, at a tavern
While the Sauer rocked his trout
Eternally through May rains.

Laundry-Day at Mecher

She was standing in her orchard as winds
        raced clouds over the wide August sky
ripe fruit trees enchanting beyond tireless flowers
        next to the wall and in her red hands
like kite strings the wash lines pulling
        with enormous pyjamas under full sail
shirts flew through fat plums above rock
        music blasting the deafness
of cows and mountain slopes of clean
        laundry in plastic baskets.
Progress crowds out remnants of an ancient world.
        The sun stepped through lanes of wet sheets
as her grandson strapped his din
        onto a motorbike and sped away, then we
entered the kitchen's soup smell
        to cross ourselves, passing wine bottles
and loaves of bread, heads bent wordless
        amidst the sound of spoons
until the laundry flapped a language older
        than the worn gleam of the doorway stones.

River

Moselle waters—
flow of amber through a terraced paradise
past vineyards and lambent woods
where no one recalls
how they lumber also around
banked hopes, docks askance
secrets and broken
Roman gods.

On the Autobahn

Dawn appears. Diesel smell intensifies.
Sleepiness retreats. BMWs, Ferraries growl by
so fast that death will strike new deals.
Dazed beyond the caps of peaks Italy is rumbling.

Ghosts of romantic poets beckon to the drivers
then recoil to tropical isles.
Fleetingly I become
one of their chocolate-coloured women.

This July I stare hard at the road and slip
into their word "voyage," travelling as they did
toward the leaven of lands dreamed of,
and like them, I don't arrive.

Nuns in Clierf

Impish and tranced, on the playground's
metal roundabout (where Steichen's
Family of Man steadies them in the pool
of time, on a château's ancient walls)
the nuns are windblown: streamers of heaven;
and their faces wear the sky's music
proud and majestic as the restraint
queens once displayed on bare foreheads.
Do they notice the wire fence
that confines them, do they want
to be plucked from their blessedness?
They seem as carefree as honeysuckle in the wind.
Remind me of masked children
in a costume ball—their puffy gowns,
sails, innocent and dramatic
as the epic grace of saints and their joy chaste
but eternal. Their souls open upward
away from this small Ardennes town and
the images of lovers in carnal embrace.
They flare like dark candles, preferring
sightseers to pilgrims because
it's outdated, the purity of heart
to be childlike and will one thing,
the gift of a sacred groom.

Benedictine Prayer

In the Abbey of St. Maurice, early spring,
and a young monk is bolting the cloister shop

fingering his rosary beads.
The tourists have returned to their delusions.

Bless me, forgive me God, he prays,
from a hook of my stark cell

a white hat beckons to me.
I kept it when a woman

left it behind. Another name has faded
on the black cross of a brother's grave.

We few who remain
hear falling glass rend the night,

we hear the bells shatter your belfry's eyes.
Lord, will I have to sell postcards forever,

why do I falter
given that I'm obedient and chaste?

Mists erase your holy face.
No pilgrim lit a candle today.

The woman's hat dreams at night
beside the crucifix, blanketed by my sighs.

Impressions of Vianden

Between the jade groves, the orchards' pink blooms,
spring claiming Vianden but like a mirage,

the silent play of centuries, the armoured knights
erect in glass cages and the Trinitarian monks

on donkeys bartering for Christian pilgrims
down Africa's dark womb, their white frocks

still ballooned by eternal winds: Victor Hugo,
an ancient whale swimming up the Our river,

Prioress Yolanda who has so captured virtue's light
in a hymn that her holy words spawn

this year of consumer pilgrims,
loud radios, processions of cars

and maybe a time when over the fortress court
she bounced a ball and as a flower child

hopped into romance and danced the tango
of unholy thoughts, imagine that serious girl

eloping toward life and then in the pungent
air, her nipples awakening, the eyes too,

the tourist shops along the steep narrow streets,
the old power plays between pleasure and faith

the renovated castle, the new salvation of Vianden
all together; Victor Hugo whose verses glide

into anthologies, Yolanda whose pleas
drum down cobbled trails each night and with fervour

entreat God one last time to forgive the profane.

Letter from Holland

Spring has returned—
to the clean little houses where Descartes
and other exiles lived. Last week
we took a bus-tour to Luxembourg,
our dead homeland. We wandered
through the empty cities,
covered with anti-radiation suits—
the ones we should have bought,
should have worn, protesting
before the fields were withered,
villages deserted, woods forever charred.
Fifteen years have passed since evacuation,
and it's still painful to think
that before the melt-down at Cattenon
we failed to object
when fat-bellied politicians sold us
tangles of fictions, litanies of lies.
Now in the Dutch museums,
near the canals, I recall meeting
summer evenings my Anita
in the Petrus gorge below ramparts
the colour of jade, and
later her head maimed, then shot
by her own hand. We should have
emigrated to America. My school chum,
installed in California, kept writing
come. We should have listened,
started a new life where children sing
in houses with windows open
to surprise. Here in Holland,
there is only orderliness, no sublime.

Venerable Meals

When crystal flasks, silver trays (in Old World
banquets with truffled goose liver, champagnes)
cajole the flagging hunger and thirst,
there appears, enfolded in time's long scarves,
temperate, becalmed,
my grandmother, the peasant matriarch,
with her dark blue apron, eating slowly
a frugal meal—the sun's fire still lingering
in the apples baked over vine embers
on her kitchen's woodstove, when inside the body
it's December and ice covers the soul.

In Canada—with monastic repasts,
not culinary triumphs—I recall the choreography
of opulent feasts in Luxembourg today.
How elegant tureens cradling venison
or pewter dishes loaded with marzipan
make me long for my grandmother.
How those ceremonious suppers also
transpose me to the table
of my snowed-in cedar house where
earth, wind, water enter
human dreams through simple fare.

VI
TWILIGHT TOCCATAS

Twilight Toccatas

Canada, on the way home from school,
past the cobblers, jewellers of the Luxembourg town,
always swept their minds—
When Josette was thirteen or fourteen
she and Martine would fire pistols at family life,
as drizzle soaked their heads outside the bakery,
and plot itineraries for departure from these low skies.

For years after, caught up in chatter,
Josette lived placidly and smoothly
as school mistress and wife,
and one day walking into the smell of bread
the eternity inside her broke up,
she hardly could keep her hand to a book,
so when the April rains came
and brought vapid days
and crocuses in the meadows,
she finally imagined Martine's life in New Brunswick,
extricating herself from an existence
where it had always been Lent.

ooooo

Love exercises: "Am I at the centre
of the world?" Martine asks herself
while she cooks breakfast near Fundy Bay.
"Martine," her husband the painter calls,
warming himself against her name.
"The logs are alive in your hands,"
says Martine. "Yellow birch," Bob answers.
"Is it light and resonant like the centre
of the world?" she asks and he smiles:
"Warmth, tenderness, plenitude."

ooooo

The Atlantic below the ramparts
pounds: gale-whips entering
the fog blankets that wrap the woods,
their house. They live musically
in each other's company, bake bread,
the blinds open at night. In bed,
no secrets, the sea holds them, and each dream
a cup of hot chocolate to be sipped,
while sleeping soundly
under a down quilt.
At dawn they jog on the beach.

ooooo

Claude paces up and down his study.
To Josette her husband's steps say "culture,"
"authority." She has some awe of him
when he speaks in quotations.
Neither knows anymore that evenings
can be spent together without agony.
And there is the melancholy of distance:
spectator of one's spouse, of one's own life.

ooooo

After Pentecost Josette steps out of somber clouds.
A new perspective to be discovered in spring,
looking through a Dutch painting's door and wondering
if the mistress and servant act out their lives.
Josette thinks she has posed as a matron for years.
Her husband hunts ideas and diseases. She fades
briefly into her neglected strength,
goes shopping for jeans instead of dresses,
as if to say, I'm a Cinderella now,
not a grande dame, lost in Luxembourg dullness.

ooooo

Claude, cigarette in hand, repeats with urgency
Turgenev's advice to Tolstoy: "Do not let life
slip through your fingers," and thinks,
"those Canadians are the royalty of bores,
their spiritual life is grey, dull."
Scene in a Luxembourg restaurant: two couples
celebrating a reunion over supper,
the men meeting for the first time, the women
reminiscing about their girlhood,
running back and forth to post-war days.
"I rather feel," Bob adds, still lingering
at home inside the painting he started
before this trip, "that light
and colour invent our lives."
Poached apples with French brandy
on dark blue plates. "Well,"
Claude says, "I prefer thinking
fists and rolled-up sleeves."

ooooo

Bob writes to Alex Colville: "We're fighting
with the beast, European culture. Does it exist?
Supplication for preserving art and nature
can be read everywhere and I study
the Dutch masters for whom
animals are elements of a tame Arcadia,
whereas in your paintings the dogs,
horses and birds still explode with the magic
of death and innocence. Are your human figures
longing for this forsaken power
of the beast when they hide their faces,
the visible sign of difference?
Lasting out their lives without shame?"

ooooo

Bob and Martine yearn for New Brunswick,
its silences, its voice inhabited
by marshes and woods.
Martine populates the Luxembourg rivers
and hills with Canadian heroes and gods.
The Europeans appear enamoured
with refined corruptions. A music
she no longer understands. Like Hölderlin
who lost his words, became a carpenter,
wrote "poetically man dwells." His fingers
speaking with the wood.

ooooo

Ears strained toward the sounds of a military band,
their eyes travel between outdoor tables
at the Place d'Armes, watching the energy
that rises from chic women, sophisticated men.
Bob feasts on orgies of Luxembourgish phrases.
Martine bites into a liqueur bonbon. Is language
always the voice of other people's masks?
Above them the sky is a canvas smeared
with huge clouds. Fifteen miles south on the Moselle,
Europe's largest nuclear plant
puffs up France's gift to its tiny neighbour.
You feel sirens in the air, feet pound toward
underground shelters. And Bob thinks,
I'll make a tapestry of this in New Brunswick.

ooooo

Josette returns home from the gynecologist.
Claude sits near the window bent over
a book, immersed in Chekhov's polished prose.
She looks at him sadly: "I haven't lived yet,
our life drains me, drives me to despair."
Claude recites from *The Duel* and
*The Notebooks: In married life the main thing
is patience. Not love. Love can't last long.*
Josette responds: "I won't have anymore
of those tedious speeches." *A woman needs
a bedroom first of all. Not honour and indulgence . . .*
In the bathroom Josette sticks a patch
of hormones on her thighs, thinking,
he sits there an empty-eyed icon.
*If you're afraid of loneliness, do not marry . . .
An unfaithful wife is a large cold cutlet
which one does not want to touch
because someone else has had it in his hands.*
"Preposterous," she murmurs, "I won't
threaten you with becoming a nun."
It dawns on him that he might not
be an indispensable part of her boudoir.
*To get married without love is just as base
and unworthy as to serve Mass without believing.*

ooooo

Josette listens to the traffic outside
and wonders why he married her.
She longs to embrace a lover,
ward off fatigues, duties, grief.
She wants to laugh and sob at once,
be alive in a bittersweet dream.
Looking up again, Claude reads,
In searching for the truth, men take two steps forward
and one backward. Suffering and the tedium of life
thrust them back, but the thirst for the truth,
and a stubborn will drive them on and on.

ooooo

The two couples find each other
one last time in the Ardennes forests,
holding out scraps of sentences to each other.
Martine's hands, still in Bruges, touch
the blond hair of a Memling angel.
Claude thinks of Russian books, men clutching
women, then flogging them with deaf fury.
Josette already lives autumn on her skin,
rains erasing summer suns, bronzing the trees.
Bob knows that the vinegar and ash
of these old cultures will pursue him even at home.
They walk off miles of sadness,
the desire not to give up lifting
out of their ordinary lives.
They rest in a country inn: hot soup, cold beer.
On the drive back to town, long views
of hedgerows, castles and twilit fields.

NOTES

PAGE

35-40   These poems have grown out of twenty years of dialogue—live and epistolary—with this Luxembourgish artist friend.

61   *"Et war esou em d'Paischten / 't stung alles an der Bléi"* (It was around Pentecost and everything was in bloom), the beginning of Michel Rodange's epic poem, *Renert*.

91   Namurs, the most famous pâtisserie in Luxembourg City.

100   Cattenon, the largest atomic plant in Europe, erected by France within sight of the Luxembourg border. In case of serious accident the entire country of Luxembourg would be irreparably destroyed.

ACKNOWLEDGEMENTS

Some of these poems have appeared or are to appear in their present form or in altered versions in the following publications: *Amethyst Review, Les Cahiers Luxembourgeois, Canadian Author, The Pittsburgh Quarterly, The Cormorant, Estuaires, Prairie Schooner, Queen's Quarterly, Reflets du Lycée Hubert Clement 1990-91, Tickle Ace, Tidepool, Tower, White Wall Review, Women's Education des Femmes, The Fiddlehead, The Windsor Review, Northern Woman Journal.*

"Life with Mother," "Mama," "Benedictine Prayer" won first prize in the *Amethyst Review*'s Poverty Contest.

"Rimbaud in Sackville" received second prize in the Writers' Federation of New Brunswick's 1994 Poetry Contest.

Dream Museum won Honourable Mention in the Alfred Bailey Category of the Writers' Federation of New Brunswick's 1994 Literary Competition.

Special thanks to Richard Lemm and Nic Weber for their editorial advice and friendship.

Cover art by Ginette Knaff.
FRONT: MONOTYPE ET COLLAGE, 1992.
BACK: *Life in another language*, MONOTYPE, 1992.

Photographs of artwork by Marc Schmit

Photograph of the author by Cyril Welch

Critics on *Life in Another Language*

RECIPIENT OF THE 1992 BRESSANI PRIZE FOR POETRY

". . . elegant and superbly polished . . . concerned with those exciting and potentially subversive boundary areas between human and divine, prose and poetry, art and everyday life, physical and spiritual experience."

—JANICE FIAMENGO, *Canadian Literature*

". . . a bright devotion to the natural world, companionship, teaching, the arts (including the culinary), mastery of skills such as mountain climbing, and travel in older cultures."

—RICHARD LEMM, *The Cormorant*

"*Life in Another Language* transforms reading into a peak experience."

—JOSY BRAUN, *Tageblatt*

". . . thought-provoking, touching, insightful—a sophisticated reflection on aspects of being alive."

—DON GUTTERIDGE

"Welch is one of the most original and interesting voices of contemporary Canadian Literature."

—ANNA FOSCHI, *L'Eco D'Italia*

"Welch has produced some of the most remarkable poetry to ever come out of this region."

—MICHAEL O. NOWLAN, *The Atlantic Advocate*

ABOUT THE AUTHOR

PHOTO: *Cyril Welch*

Liliane Welch was born in Luxembourg. She studied in Europe and in the United States and immigrated to Canada in 1967. Welch has received many literary awards, including the Bressani and Alfred Bailey prizes. Her poems have been widely anthologized and translated into German, French and Italian. Liliane Welch teaches at Mount Allison University and lives in Sackville, New Brunswick.